2 Be Extraordinary Today!

365 MOTIVATIONAL QUOTES TO START YOUR DAY

Compiled by Tracy Rosa

Pegasus Publication

Tracy Rosa/Pegasus Entertainment
West Lafayette, IN

Book Layout © 2016 BookDesignTemplates.com

2 Be Extraordinary Today! / Tracy Rosa
ISBN 978-1-6895883-4-8

Do just once what others say you can't.
Paulo Coelho

~~~

*Definiteness of purpose is the starting
point of all achievement.
W. Clement Stone*

~~~

Optimism is the faith that leads to
achievement. Nothing can be done
without hope and confidence.
Helen Keller

~~~

*The past cannot be changed, and the
future is yet in your power, so live for
today.
Unknown*

~~~

Every exit is an entry somewhere else.
Tom Stoppard

If you really believe in your dreams,
you will see opportunities, not
obstacles in making them come to a
reality.
Wayne Dyer

~~~

*Your talent is God's gift to you, what you
do with it is your gift back.
Leo Buscaglia*

~~~

If you happened to fall down
yesterday, then stand yourself back up
today.
H.G. Wells

~~~

The will to win, the desire to succeed,
the urge to reach your full potential are
the keys that will unlock the door to
your excellence.
Confucius
~~~

*There is only one corner of the universe
you can be certain of improving and that
is your own self.*
Aldous Huxley

~~~

Act as if what you do makes a
difference, because it does.
William James

~~~

*Look up at the stars and not down at
your feet. try to make sense of what you
see and wonder about what makes the
universe exist.*
Stephen Hawking

~~~

Do the difficult things while they are
easy and do the great things while they
are still small.
Lao Tzu
~~~

Be miserable or motivate yourself to be happy, whatever has to be done is always your choice.
Wayne Dyer

~~~

Things do not just happen. They are made to happen.
John F. Kennedy

~~~

Permanence, perseverance, and persistence in spite of all obstacles, discouragement, and impossibilities: It is this, that in all things that distinguishes the strong soul from the weak.
Thomas Carlyle

~~~

Success means doing the best we can with what we have. It is in the doing, in the trying, in reaching for the highest personal standard.
Zig Ziglar
~~~

Hard times don't create heroes. It is during the hard times when the hero within us is revealed.
Bob Riley

~~~

Your mind is a powerful thing. Believe you can and you're halfway there.
Theodore Roosevelt

~~~

Start by doing what's necessary, then do what's possible and suddenly you are doing the impossible.
Francis of Assisi

~~~

I attribute my success to the fact that I never gave or took any excuse.
Florence Nightingale
~~~

Whatever you hold in your mind on a consistent basis is exactly what you will experience in your life.
Tony Robbins

~~~

I am not a product of my circumstances, but of the decisions I make.
Stephen Covey

~~~

The future belongs to those who believe in the beauty of their dreams.
Franklin Roosevelt

~~~

Perseverance is the hard work you do after you get tired of doing the hard work you already did.
Newt Gingrich
~~~

Most of the important things in the world have been accomplished by people who have kept on trying when there seemed to be no hope left.
Dale Carnegie

~~~

Knowing is not enough, we must apply. Willing is not enough, we must do.
Johann von Goethe

~~~

Don't be pushed around by the fears in your mind instead be led by the dreams of your heart.
Roy T. Bennett

~~~

It is during the darkest moments that we must focus the hardest to see the light.
Aristotle Onassis
~~~

Only through experience of trial and suffering can the soul be strengthened, vision cleared, ambition inspired, and success achieved.
Helen Keller

~~~

You are here to enrich the world and you impoverish yourself if you forget that errand.
Woodrow Wilson

~~~

Don't be afraid to leap with your whole heart, for a safety net will always appear.
John Burroughs

~~~

The more man meditates upon good thoughts, the better be his world and the world at large.
Confucius
~~~

If you don't like how things are,
change it. You are not a tree.
Jim Rohn

~~~

*Ever tried, ever failed, no matter, try
again, fail again, but fail better next
time.*
Samuel Beckett

~~~

You simply have to put one foot in
front of the other and keep going by
wearing blinders and plowing straight
ahead.
George Lucas

~~~

*Do you want to know who you are? Don't
ask! Act! Action will delineate and define
you.*
Thomas Jefferson
~~~

*The ultimate aim of the ego is not to see
something but to be something
Muhammed Iqbal*

~~~

Be impeccable with your word. Speak
out with integrity and use the power of
your word in the direction of love and
truth.
Don Miguel Ruiz

~~~

*Gratefulness, there is always more to be
thankful for.
Tyler Green*

~~~

For any problem no matter how big or
complex it may be, there is always a
solution.
Earl Nightingale
~~~

*There is no passion to be found playing
small, or in settling for a life that is less
than the one you are capable of living.*
Nelson Mandela

~~~

One way to keep momentum going is
to have consistently greater goals.
Michael Korda

~~~

*Tough times never last, but tough people
do.*
Robert Schuller

~~~

Hard work always beats talent when
talent doesn't work hard.
Tim Notke
~~~

Positive types see opportunities, for each day is a new beginning with new possibilities and new experiences.
Sullins Stuart

~~~

Learn as if you were not reaching your goals and also, as though you were scared of missing them.
Confucius

~~~

Don't stop when you are tired, stop when you are done.
Unknown

~~~

The demarcation between a positive and a negative desire or action is not whether it gives you an immediate feeling but whether it ultimately results in positive or negative consequences.
Dalai Lama
~~~

Success seems to be connected with
action. successful people keep moving,
they make mistakes, but they don't
quit.
Conrad Hilton

~~~

A man can be as great as he wants to be
if he is willing to sacrifice the little
things in life and pay the price for the
things that are worthwhile.
Vince Lombardi

~~~

*Every great story happened because
someone decided not to give up but kept
on going no matter what.*
Spryte Loriano

~~~

Ideas without action are worthless,
they are just thoughts drifting in space.
Harvey Mackay
~~~

When it is obvious that the goal cannot be reached, don't adjust the goal, adjust the action plan.
Confucius

~~~

Successful leaders embrace the reality that their models may be wrong or incomplete. Only when we admit what we didn't know can we ever hope to learn.
Ed Catnill

~~~

Stop setting goals, for they are pure fantasy unless you have a specific plan to achieve them.
Stephen Covey

~~~

I find that the harder I work, the more luck I seem to have.
Thomas Jefferson
~~~

Little minds are tamed and subdued by misfortune, but great minds rise above it.
Washington Irving

~~~

The question is not who is going to let me but it's who is going to stop me?
Ayn Rand

~~~

Successful people do what unsuccessful people are not willing to do.
Jim Rohn

~~~

Action is the foundational key to all success.
Pablo Picasso

~~~

If you can't change your fate, then change your attitude.
Amy Tan

Joy must be developed from the inside.
If we cannot find happiness within
ourselves, we will not be able to find it
elsewhere.
Allan Lukos

~~~

*If you want to be successful, you must
respond to only one rule, don't lie to
yourself.*
Paulo Coelho

~~~

Nothing is impossible, the word itself
says I'm possible.
Audrey Hepburn

~~~

*Life begins at the end of your comfort
zone.*
Neale Walsh
~~~

Perfection is not attainable, but if we
chase it we can catch excellence.
Vince Lombardi

~~~

*The great thing is not so much where you
stand, but in what direction you are
moving.*
Oliver Wendell Holmes

~~~

Live each day as if your life had just
begun.
Johann Von Goethe

~~~

*Health is the greatest gift, contentment
the greatest wealth and faithfulness the
best relationship.*
Buddha
~~~

Let us remember one book, one pen,
one child and one teacher can change
the world.
Malala Yousafzai

~~~

*When someone says that life is hard, I'm
tempted to ask, compared to what?*
Sydney Harris

~~~

Nurture your mind with great
thoughts, to believe in heroic makes
heroes.
Benjamin Disraeli

~~~

*The real opportunity for success lies not
in the job but in the person.*
Zig Ziglar
~~~

Luck is a dividend of sweat, the more
you sweat the luckier you get.
Ray Kroc

~~~

*When I let go of what I am, I become
what I might be.
Lao Tzu*

~~~

Nothing in this world is more common
than unsuccessful people with
unfulfilled talent.
Unknown

~~~

*Success is walking from failure to failure
with no loss of enthusiasm.
Winston Churchill*
~~~

No matter where you go, wherever
you go, whatever the weather may be,
always bring your own sunshine.
Anthony D'Angelo

~~~

*Success is a state of mind. If you want it,
start thinking of yourself as successful.
Dr. Joyce Brothers*

~~~

Don't aim for success, if you want it,
just do what you love and believe in
and the rest will come naturally.
David Frost

~~~

*Figure out what your destiny in life is,
then simply go and do it.
Henry Ford*
~~~

Press forward, do not stop, do not
linger in your journey, but strive for
the mark set up before you.
George Whitefield

~~~

*Remember that not getting what you
want is sometimes a wonderful stroke of
luck.*
Dalai Lama

~~~

Do not wait, the time will never be just
right. Start where you stand and work
with whatever tools you have at your
command, and better tools will be
found as you go along.
George Herbert

~~~

Coming together is a beginning.
Keeping together is progress. Working
together is success.
Henry Ford
~~~

*Success only happens to those who dare
to attempt.*
Mallika Tripathi

~~~

The true meaning of life is to plant
trees under whose shade you do not
expect to sit.
Nelson Henderson

~~~

*It is not what you loudly say from your
mouth that determines your life, but it's
what you whisper inside of your head
that has the most power.*
Robert Kiyosaki

~~~

There will be obstacles, there will be
doubters there will be mistakes, but
with hard work, there are no limits.
Michael Phelps
~~~

Change your life today. Don't gamble on the future, act now, without delay.
Simone De Beauvoir

~~~

Never give up for that is just the place and time that the tide will turn.
Harriet Stow

~~~

You are braver than you believe, stronger than you seem and smarter than you think.
Christopher Robbin

~~~

The man who has confidence in himself gains the confidence of others.
Hasidic Proverb
~~~

Nothing can stop the man with the right mental attitude from achieving his goal, and nothing on earth can help the man with the wrong attitude.
Thomas Jefferson

~~~

Never allow a person to tell you 'no' who doesn't have the power to say 'yes'.
Eleanor Roosevelt

~~~

Imagination is everything. It is the preview of life's coming attractions.
Albert Einstein

~~~

Try not. Do or do not, there is no try.
Master Yoda
~~~

You attract what you are, not what you want. If you want great, then be great.
Kushan wisdom

~~~

Falling down is an accident but staying down is a choice.
Unknown

~~~

If you have the power to make someone happy, do it. The world needs more of that.
Anonymous

~~~

Don't be afraid to give up the good life and go for a greater one.
Steve Prefontaine
~~~

Life's greatest lessons are usually learned at the worst times and from the worst mistakes.
Confucius

~~~

The key to success is to focus our conscious mind on the things we desire, not things we fear.
Brian Tracy

~~~

Someday is not a day of the week.
Janet Dailey

~~~

Don't count the days, instead make the days count.
Muhammed Ali
~~~

You get to decide where your time is spent. You can either spend it moving forward or putting out fires and if you don't decide, then others will always turn you into a firefighter.
Tony Morgan

~~~

Never give up on a dream just because of the time it will take to accomplish it. The time will pass anyway.
Earl Nightingale

~~~

Don't quit. You're already in pain. You're already hurting. So get a reward from it.
Bill Belichek

~~~

If we keep doing what we're doing, we're going to keep getting what we're getting.
Stephen Covey
~~~

*Do what you have to do until you can do
what you want to do.*
Oprah Winfrey

~~~

The man on top of the mountain didn't
fall there. He climbed there.
Vince Lombardi

~~~

*A year from now you may have wished
you had started to pursue your dreams
today.*
Karen Lamb

~~~

When someone tells me 'no', it doesn't
mean 'I can't do it', it simply means 'I
can't do it with them'.
Karen Miller
~~~

If one advances confidently in the direction of his dreams and endeavors to live a life which he has imagined, then he will meet with success.
Henry David Thoreau

~~~

The individual who says it is not possible should just move out of the way of those who are doing it.
Tricia Cunningham

~~~

Work until your idols become your rivals.
Drake

~~~

Between stimulus and response is our greatest power, the freedom of choice.
Stephen Covey
~~~

If you don't build your dream, someone
else will hire you to help build theirs.
Tony Gaskins

~~~

Be stubborn about your goals but be
flexible about your methods.
Tim Notke

~~~

Don't be pushed by your problems,
instead be led by your dreams.
Ralph Waldo Emerson

~~~

If everything seems under control,
you're not moving fast enough.
Mario Andretti
~~~

Strive to go as far as you can see, when you get there, you'll be able to see even further.
Thomas Carlyle

~~~

A sailboat's rudder is useless while the sails are down. Set sail, get going. You can't get where you want without the tools you need.
Max Lucado

~~~

The future depends on what you do today.
Mahatma Gandhi

~~~

People often say that motivation doesn't last, neither does bathing, which is why it is recommended daily.
Zig Ziglar
~~~

Don't wait on perfect conditions for success to happen, just go ahead and do something.
Dan Miller

~~~

People will forget what you did, what you said, but they will never forget how you made them feel.
Maya Angelou

~~~

Complaining about a problem without posing a solution is called whining.
Teddy Roosevelt

~~~

It is during our failures that we discover our true desire to succeed.
Kevin Ngo
~~~

*Aim to be in the company of the
immortals.*
David Ogilvy

~~~

When you face your fears, most of the
time you will discover that it was not
really such a big threat after all.
Les Brown

~~~

*There are no secrets to success. It is the
result of preparation, hard work and
learning from failure.*
Colin Powell

~~~

New beginnings are often disguised as
painful endings.
Lao Tzu
~~~

*What seems to us as bitter trials are
often blessings in disguise.*
Oscar Wilde

~~~

*You're 100% responsible for your life, so
stop complaining and make something of
it.*
Mathieu Fortin

~~~

Be so good they can't ignore you.
Steve Martin

~~~

When you think, you are only
repeating what you already know but if
you listen you may learn something
new.
Dalai Lama
~~~

When you feel like quitting, always think back for the reason you got started.
Dr. Joyce Brothers

~~~

Success all depends on the second letter in this sentence.
Unknown

~~~

When you go in search of honey, you must expect to be stung by a few bees.
Christopher Robbins

~~~

We must all learn to work hard, handle rejection and be outside our comfort zone.
George Arzuaga
~~~

Hope is brightest when it dawns from fear.
Walter Scott

~~~

Your best days are still out in front of you.
Joel Osteen

~~~

To be yourself in a world that is constantly trying to make you something else is the greatest accomplishment.
Ralph Waldo Emerson

~~~

Make each day a masterpiece.
John Wooden

~~~

A ship is always safest ashore, but that is not what it's built for.
Unknown

Don't simply go through life but grow
through life.
Eric Butterworth

~~~

*Live as if you were to die tomorrow and
learn as if you were to live forever.
Unknown*

~~~

The first step to success is taken when
you refuse to be a captive to the
environment you find yourself in.
Mark Casia

~~~

*Purpose is something for which one is
responsible. It is not divinely assigned.
Michael J. Fox*
~~~

Imagine no limitations; decide what's right and desirable before you decide what is possible.
Brian Tracy

~~~

If you can't outplay them, then outwork them.
Ben Hogan

~~~

Quietly expect great things to happen, and no doubt they will.
Zelda Fitzgerald

~~~

Only you have the power to determine whether your future mimics your past.
Skip Pritchard
~~~

Enthusiasm is the yeast that makes
your hopes shine to the stars.
Henry Ford

~~~

*Wisdom is the reward for surviving our
own stupidity.
Brian Rathborne*

~~~

Life isn't about getting and having, but
it's about giving and being.
Kevin Kruse

~~~

*Don't ever let someone tell you that you
can't do something. You have your
dream to protect, so go and make it.
Will Smith*
~~~

Not everyone will understand your journey. That's fine. It's not their journey to make sense of. It's yours.
Zero Dean

~~~

You can never ride the wave that came in and went out yesterday.
John Wannamaker

~~~

I've learned that something constructive comes from every defeat.
Tom Landry

~~~

Train your mind to see the good things in life and everything. Positivity is a choice the happiness of your life depends on the quality of your thoughts.
Marcan Dangel
~~~

*A diamond is a chunk of coal that did
well under pressure.*
Henry Kissinger

~~~

The only limits you have are the limits
you believe.
Wayne Dyer

~~~

*Only put off tomorrow what you are
willing to die having left undone.*
Pablo Picasso

~~~

Whoever is trying to bring you down
is already below you.
Brian Tracy

*Don't downgrade your dream just to fit
your reality. Upgrade your conviction to
match your destiny.*
Jim Rohn
~~~

What if I fail? Oh, but what if I fly?
Erin Hanson

~~~

Stop chasing the money and start chasing the passion in your life.
Tony Hsieh

~~~

Fall seven times and stand up eight.
Japanese Proverb

~~~

All progress takes place outside the comfort zone.
Michael J. Bobak

~~~

Whatever your situation might be, set your mind to it with a great attitude and you're halfway to success.
Bethany Hamilton

The past should stay in the past, for it can destroy the future life for what tomorrow has to offer, not for what yesterday has taken away.
Anonymous

Love is the absence of judgment.
Dalai Lama

~~~

Only as high as I reach can I grow, only as far as I seek can I go, only as deep as I look can I see, only as much as I dream can I be.
Karen Raun

~~~

No greater achiever, even those who made it seem easy ever succeeded without hard work.
Jonathan Sacks

The highest reward for a man's toil is
not what he gets for it but what he
becomes by it.
John Ruskin

~~~

There are no shortcuts to any place
worth going.
Beverly Sills

~~~

You were hired because you met some
expectations, but you will be promoted
by exceeding them.
Saji Ljlyemi

~~~

None of us is as smart as all of us.
Ken Blanchard
~~~

Life isn't about finding yourself, but
about creating yourself.
George Bernard Shaw

~~~

*We must have a theme or a goal for the
purpose of our lives, for if we don't know
where we are aiming, we will never hit
the goal.
Mary Kay Ash*

~~~

You don't get the same moment again
in life, so make the most of it.
Unknown

~~~

*The most beautiful things in the world
cannot be seen or even touched but felt
with the heart.
Helen Keller*
~~~

It takes two flints to make a fire.
Louisa May Alcott

~~~

You don't get harmony when everybody
sings the same note.
Doug Floyd

~~~

The strength of the team is each
individual member, but the strength of
each member is the team.
Phil Jackson

~~~

So powerful is the light of unity that it
can illuminate the whole earth.
Bahaullah

~~~

Even if you are on the right track,
you'll get run over if you just sit there.
Will Rogers

*Fear is contagious, but so is hope,
dreams, compassion, and love.*
T. E. Rosa

~~~

Strength and growth come only
through continuous effort and struggle.
Napoleon Hill

~~~

*Every action we take, everything we do is
either a victory or a defeat in the struggle
to become what we want to be.*
Ninon de L'Enclos

~~~

If there is no struggle, there is no
progress.
Frederick Douglass
~~~

You're allowed to scream and even cry,
but never to give up.
Anonymous

~~~

Experience satisfaction but never
become satisfied.
Jim Lynch

~~~

The road to success is dotted with many
tempting parking spots.
Will Rogers

~~~

If you think you are too small to make
a difference be thankful you are not a
mosquito.
Dalai Lama
~~~

*A word of encouragement during failure
is worth more than an hour of praise
after success.*
Unknown

~~~

Without the rain in your life, there
would be no enjoying the sight of a
rainbow.
Gilbert Chesterton

~~~

*To live is to express and to express, you
have to create. Creation is never merely
repetition to live is to express freely in
creation.*
Bruce Lee

~~~

*It always seems impossible until you do
it.*
Nelson Mandela
~~~

Life is no brief candle. It is a sort of splendid torch which I have got a hold of for just a moment and it burns as brightly as possible before it is handed away for future generations.
George Bernard Shaw

~~~

While you were struggling, you never thought that you would be glad that you never gave up during that period of your life.
Brittany Burgunder

~~~

You must never be fearful about what you are doing when it is the right thing to do.
Rosa Parks

~~~

Strive not to be a success, but rather to be of value.
Albert Einstein
~~~

The best revenge is massive success.
Frank Sinatra

~~~

*Have no fear of perfection, for you will
never find it.*
Salvador Dali

~~~

If you cannot get rid of the family
skeleton, then you may as well try to
make it dance.
George Bernard Shaw

~~~

*Life is essentially an endless series of
problems. The solution to one problem is
merely the creation of the next one.
Don't hope for a life without problems,
there is no such thing. Instead, hope for a
life full of good problems.*
Mark Manson
~~~

Don't think about it, just do it.
Horace

~~~

The first step toward success is taken when you refuse to be a captive of the environment in which you find yourself.
Mark Caine

~~~

Never complain and never explain, just keep plugging along.
Benjamin Disraeli

~~~

Nobody can go back and start over with a new beginning, but anyone can start today and make a new ending.
Unknown
~~~

It is time for us to stand and cheer for the doer, the achiever, the one who recognizes the challenges and does something about it.
Vince Lombardi

~~~

Sometimes the questions are complicated while the answers are simple.
Dr. Seuss

~~~

Be willing to sacrifice what you think you have today for the life that you want tomorrow.
Neil Strauss

~~~

What lies behind you and what lies in front of you pales in comparison to what lies inside of you.
Ralph Waldo Emerson
~~~

The one thing that you have that nobody else has is you. Your voice, your mind, your story, your vision, so write and draw and build and play and sing and dance and live as only you can.
Neil Gaiman

~~~

You will never do anything in this world without courage. It is the greatest quality in the mind, next to honor.
Aristotle

~~~

Plan to take off, don't just sit on the runway and hope someone will come along and fly the airplane.
Donald Trump

He who refuses to embrace a unique
opportunity loses the prize as surely as
if he had failed.
William James

~~~

When one door closes another opens but
we so often look so long and so
regretfully upon the closed door, that we
do not see the one which has been opened
for us.
Alexander Graham Bell

~~~

Very little is needed to make a happy
life. It's all within yourself in the way
of your thinking.
Marcus Aurelius

~~~

In the end, it's not the years in your life
that count but it's the life in your years.
Abraham Lincoln
~~~

I love the man that can smile in trouble, that can gather strength from distress and grow brave by reflection.
Thomas Paine

~~~

We are all in the gutter, but some of us are looking up at the stars.
Oscar Wilde

~~~

Be who you are and say what you feel because those who mind don't matter and those who matter don't mind.
Dr. Seuss

~~~

Accept no definition of your life but define yourself instead.
Harvey Fierstein
~~~

If you set your goals ridiculously high
and it's a failure, you will find yourself
high above everyone else's success.
James Cameron

~~~

*One day your life will flash before your
eyes so make sure it's worth watching.
Gerard Way*

~~~

Sometimes you don't realize your own
strength until you come face to face
with your greatest weakness.
Susan Gale

~~~

*Difficulties are meant to rouse, not to
discourage. The human spirit is to grow
stronger by conflict.
William Channing*
~~~

Make up your mind that no matter what comes your way, no matter how difficult, how unfair, you will do more than simply survive but you will thrive in spite of it.
Joel Osteen

~~~

Never regret a day in your life, good days give you happiness and bad days give you experience.
Unknown

~~~

Those who don't believe in magic will never find it.
Ronald Dahl

~~~

Accept responsibility for your life, because it is you who will get you where you want to go. No one else.
Les Brown
~~~

It is not about how hard you can hit,
but how hard you can get hit and keep
moving forward.
Rocky Balboa

~~~

*There are two ways of exerting your
strength by either pushing down or by
pulling up.*
Booker T Washington

~~~

A truly strong person does not need
the approval of the weak person to do
greatness.
Vernon Howard

~~~

*He who believes in himself is strong, who
doubts is weak. Strong convictions
precede great actions.*
Louisa May Alcott
~~~

Challenges are what make life
interesting and overcoming them is
what makes life meaningful.
Joshua Marine

~~~

*There is no elevator to success, you must
take the stairs for it to be sustainable.
Anonymous*

~~~

We generate fears while we sit and we
overcome them by action.
Dr. Henry Link

~~~

*If you don't like the road you're walking
on then start paving another one.
Dolly Parton*
~~~

The most beautiful things in the world
cannot be seen or touched but only felt
by the heart.
Helen Keller

~~~

Until you cross the bridge of your
insecurities you can't begin to explore
your possibilities.
Tim Fargo

~~~

*Strength does not come from winning.
Your struggles to win develop your
strength. It's when you go through the
hardships and decide not to surrender
that is strength.*
Arnold Schwarzenegger

~~~

The world will break everyone and
afterward some are stronger at the
broken places.
Ernest Hemingway
~~~

*You may not realize it at the time, but
sometimes a kick in the teeth may be the
best thing in the world for you.*
Walt Disney

~~~

Don't be overwhelmed in life because
life is just a series of baby steps.
Hoda Kotb

~~~

*Love yourself first and then everything
else will fall into place.*
Lucille Ball

~~~

Lead from the heart, not the head.
Princess Diana

~~~

*Don't give it five minutes if you are not
willing to give it five years.*
Meghan Markle

What comes easy won't last long, and
what lasts long won't come easy.
Unknown

~~~

Imagination is the only weapon in the
war against reality.
Lewis Carroll

~~~

*It is better to walk alone than with a
crowd going in the wrong direction.
Herman Siv*

~~~

If the plan isn't working, change the
plan but keep the focus on the goal the
plan was meant to reach.
Tony Robbins
~~~

I will breathe, I will think of solutions, I will not let my worry control me, I will not let my stress level break me. I will simply breathe, and it will be okay because I will never quit.
Shayne McClendon

~~~

To succeed in life you need three things, a wishbone, a funny bone, and a backbone.
Reba McIntire

~~~

The biggest adventure you can take is to live your life as you dream it.
Oprah Winfrey

~~~

The most important, persistent and urgent question in life is what are we doing for others?
Martin Luther King
~~~

*I've failed over and over and over again
in life and that is why I have succeeded.*
Michael Jordan

~~~

One of the happiest moments in life is
when you find the courage to let go of
what you can't change.
Maya Angelou

~~~

If you don't go after what you want,
you'll never get it. If you don't ask, the
answer will always be 'no' and if you
don't step forward you will always be
stuck in the same place.
Anonymous

~~~

*You can't start reading the next chapter
in your life if you keep re-reading the last
chapter.*
Les Brown
~~~

Sometimes you will never know the value of a moment until it becomes a memory.
Dr. Seuss

~~~

Every day may not be good but there is something good in every day.
Confucius

~~~

It is not what we have in life that matters but who we have in our lives that truly matters the most.
Margaret Laurence

~~~

One day or day one, it is your decision when procrastination ends.
Mark Twain
~~~

Small steps in the right direction can
turn out to be the biggest step of your
life.
Unknown

~~~

The most beautiful people wear their
hearts on their sleeves and their souls in
their smiles.
Mark Anthony

~~~

The meaning of life is to find your gift,
while the purpose of life is to give it
away.
William Shakespeare

~~~

Let us endeavor so to live our lives so that
when we die even the undertaker will be
sorry.
Mark Twain
~~~

Don't let what you cannot do interfere
with what you can do.
John Wooden

~~~

*If everything was perfect you would never
learn, and you would never grow.
Beyonce*

~~~

Education is the greatest most
powerful weapon which you can use to
change the world.
Nelson Mandela

~~~

Wake at dawn with a winged heart and
give thanks for another day of loving.
Kahlil Gibran
~~~

*Lighthouses don't go running all over the
island looking for boats to save. They
stay in one spot and shine brightly.*
Anne Lamont

~~~

You can discover more about a man in
one hour of play than in an entire day
of conversation.
Plato

~~~

*Kindness is the language which the deaf
can hear and the blind can see.*
Mark Twain

~~~

If you genuinely want something, don't
wait for it, teach yourself to be
impatient.
Gurbaksh Chahal
~~~

Success does not consist in never
making mistakes but in never making
the same one a second time.
George Bernard Shaw

~~~

*You've got to get up every morning with
determination if you're going to go to bed
with satisfaction at the end of the day.*
George Lorimer

~~~

Real difficulties can be overcome, it is
only the imaginary ones that are really
unconquerable.
Theodore Vail

~~~

*Man is most uniquely human when he
turns obstacles into opportunities.*
Eric Hoffen
~~~

A teacher affects eternity and can
never tell where that influence stops.
Henry Adams

~~~

Happiness is not something you
postpone for the future, but it is
something you design for the present.
Jim Rohn

~~~

All appears to change when we change.
Henri Amiel

~~~

Man's main task is to give birth to
himself to become what he potentially
is, the most important product of his
effort is his own personality.
Erich Fromm
~~~

*There is no traffic jam along the extra
mile taken by the few.*
Roger Staubach

~~~

Discouragement and failure are two of
the surest stepping stones to success.
Dale Carnegie

~~~

The successful warrior is the average
man with laser-like focus.
Bruce Lee

~~~

There are two kinds of people in this
world who will tell you that you can't
succeed. Those who are afraid to try
and those who are afraid you'll
succeed.
Ray Goforth
~~~

*Until you make peace with who you are,
you'll never be content with what you
have.*
Doris Mortman

~~~

Opportunity keeps knocking at the
least opportune moments.
Ducharme

~~~

*Some people think it's holding on that
makes them strong but sometimes it's
letting go.*
Sylvia Robinson

~~~

The greatest victory is over one's fears.
Dhamnapodi

~~~

Where hope is hungry, everyone feeds it.
Mignon McLaughlin

You may only succeed if you desire succeeding; you may only fail if you do not mind failing.
Philippos

~~~

Courage is resistance to fear, mastery of fear, not absence of fear.
Mark Twain

~~~

The function of leadership is to produce more leaders, not more followers.
Ralph Nadar

~~~

Whenever you find yourself on the side of the majority it is time to pause and reflect.
Mark Twain
~~~

*The only way most people recognize their
limits is by trespassing on them.*
Tom Morris

~~~

Edison failed 10,000 times before
perfecting the lightbulb. Don't worry if
you fail a few times.
Napoleon Hill

~~~

*We create our life by pursuing interests
that drive us and by our reaction to the
events that happen to us.*
James Rosseau

~~~

Guard well your spare moments for
they are like uncut diamonds. Discard
them and you will never know their
value.
Ralph Waldo Emerson
~~~

If you can't explain it simply, then you don't understand it well enough.
Albert Einstein

~~~

What is the point of being alive if you don't at least try to do something that's remarkable every day that scares you?
Will Smith

~~~

There is no greater gift you can give or receive than to honor your calling.
Oprah Winfrey

~~~

If you organize your life around your passion, you can turn your passion into your story and your story into something bigger, something that matters.
Blake Mycoskie
~~~

To meet your destiny, you first have to meet your purpose, a boundless, passionate energy that guides you down a path created just for you.
Dr. Oz

~~~

Don't raise your voice, improve your argument instead.
Unknown

~~~

What seems to us as bitter trials are often blessings in disguise.
Oscar Wilde

~~~

When you stop chasing the wrong things you give the right things a chance to catch you.
Lolly Daskal
~~~

The distance between insanity and genius is measured only by success.
Bruce Feirstein

~~~

No masterpiece was ever created by a lazy artist.
Unknown

~~~

The self is given by you, not given by others.
Barbara Myerhoff

~~~

Having a sense of purpose is having a sense of self. A course to plot is a destination to hope for.
Bryant McGill
~~~

'What am I living for?' and 'What am I dying for?' should be the same question.
Margaret Atwood

~~~

People who use time wisely, spend it on activities that advance their overall purpose in life.
John Maxwell

~~~

I would argue that nothing gives life more purpose than the realization that every moment of consciousness is a precious and fragile gift that should never be wasted.
Steven Pinker

~~~

If you don't value your time, neither will others. Stop giving away your time and talents and start charging for it.
Kim Garst
~~~

A successful person is one who can lay
a firm foundation with the bricks
others have thrown at him.
David Brinkley

~~~

*Great minds discuss ideas, average
minds discuss events while small minds
discuss other people.
Eleanor Roosevelt*

~~~

Just when the caterpillar thought the
world was ending, he turned into a
butterfly.
Dalai Lama

~~~

*There is no greater agony than bearing
an untold story inside you.
Maya Angelou*
~~~

Great minds have purposes while
others have wishes.
Washington Irving

~~~

*A person who never made a mistake
never tried anything new.
Albert Einstein*

~~~

To exist just for yourself is
meaningless, you can achieve the most
satisfaction when you feel related to
some greater purpose in life,
something greater than just yourself.
Denis Waitley

~~~

*If you want to achieve greatness, stop
asking for permission.
Unknown*
~~~

Trust because you are willing to accept
the risk, not because it's safe or
certain.
Anonymous

~~~

Take up one idea and make it your life,
think of it, dream of it, live on that
idea. Let your brain, muscles, nerves
and every part of your body be full of
that one idea and leave every other
idea alone.
Swami Vivekananda

~~~

*To live a creative life, we must lose our
fear of being wrong.*
Dr. Seuss

~~~

I can't change the direction of the wind
but I can adjust my sails to reach my
destination.
Jimmy Dean
~~~

A winner is a dreamer who never gave up.
Nelson Mandela

~~~

The most common way people give up
their power is by thinking that they
don't have any.
Alice Walker

~~~

*The most difficult thing to do is to act, to
get started, the rest is really tenacity.*
Amelia Earhart

~~~

Press forward and do not stop or linger
in your journey but strive for the mark
set before you.
George Whitefield
~~~

If not us, who? If not now, when?
John F Kennedy

~~~

Don't worry about failures. Worry
about the chances you miss when you
don't even try.
Jack Canfield

~~~

Every truth passes through three
stages before it is recognized, it is
ridiculed, opposed and then finally it is
regarded as self-evident.
Arthur Schopenhauer

~~~

A champion is someone who gets up
when he thinks he can't.
Jack Dempsey

~~~

The best preparation for tomorrow is
doing your very best today.
Jackson Browne

~~~

Put your heart, mind, and soul into even
your smallest acts, for this is the true
secret of success.
Swami Sivananda

~~~

Many of life's failures are people who
did not realize how close they were to
success when they gave up.
Thomas Edison

~~~

If you hear a voice within you say 'You
cannot paint' then by all means paint
and that voice will be silenced.
Vincent Van Gogh
~~~

You may find the best friend or the
worst enemy by looking in the mirror,
and the choice is solely yours.
English Proverb

~~~

*Courage is the first of human qualities
because it guarantees all other qualities.*
Winston Churchill

~~~

Keep your face always towards the
sunshine, and shadows will always fall
behind you.
Walt Whitman

~~~

*Someone is sitting in the shade today
because a tree was planted a long time
ago by someone else.*
Warren Buffett
~~~

No act of kindness, no matter how
small it may be, is ever wasted.
Aesop

Other works by Tracy Rosa

Inspirational Quotes
Be Extraordinary Today
2 Be Extraordinary Today

Novels
Tears of St. Benedict's
Kiss the Blarney Stone
A New Beginning, Again

Children's Stories
The Extraordinary, Unbelievable and Definitively Odd Adventures of Sir Reginald Arbuckle III

Stage Play Scripts
Angel Eyes the musical
The Ballad of Tucker Stump
Wizard of WonderOzLand
The Poet of Mt. Olympus
Valhalla Live
Wake me up! I'm not dead yet!
The Last Disciple – One Man Play
The Last Disciple – School Version
The Last Disciple – Full cast
Good night May God Bless
Downtown Dickens

Available thru Amazon.Com
Pegasuseande.com

www.ingramcontent.com/pod-product-compliance
Lightning Source LLC
Chambersburg PA
CBHW051216250726
48655CB00006B/2437